AF754066

HAJRA WAHEED

HAJRA WAHEED

Contemporary Art Museum St. Louis

WASSAN AL-KHUDHAIRI

Contents

Foreword

LISA MELANDRI

Hajra Waheed: A Solo Exhibition is the first survey of this important artist's work in the United States. Waheed's oeuvre is difficult to categorize, taking on many media—sound installation, video, painting, sculpture, and works on paper. However, regardless of form, her work is consistently engaged with the most salient issues of our time, from protest to resource extraction. In her singular and poetic way, Waheed sheds light on global histories of colonial and state violence and explores a collective, borderless future of resistance and resilience. *A Solo Exhibition* includes the seminal, major work *Hum* (2020), Waheed's multichannel sound installation, featuring eight hummed songs of protest from South, Central, and West Asia, and East and North Africa. In this powerful work, the artist manages to weave a composition of resistance in an enveloping, mesmerizing—and abstract—form that subversively immerses the listener into shared global struggle against authoritarianism and oppression. Initially created upon invitation for the Lahore Biennale 02 (2020) in Pakistan, Waheed has reimagined this work for presentation at the Contemporary Art Museum St. Louis (CAM). We are also thrilled to be able to feature a new commission, allowing audiences to experience work created especially for St. Louis.

My gratitude goes to former Ferring Foundation Chief Curator Wassan Al-Khudhairi for deftly organizing this potent and beautiful exhibition. Throughout her time at CAM, Al-Khudhairi has brought her great knowledge of the global art world to the context of St. Louis, siting salient artistic voices from afar in our local present moment. This exhibition is no different, and Waheed's work will have profound impact for the audiences in our region. My appreciation extends also to Associate Curator Misa Jeffereis for her assistance on the exhibition, as well as to the staff at CAM, who rise to every occasion with equal parts professionalism and spirit.

The exhibition is accompanied by a major publication. With contributions by Al-Khudhairi; Rayya Badran, writer and educator; and H.G. Masters, deputy editor and deputy publisher for *ArtAsiaPacific*; the catalog skillfully contextualizes Waheed's work. Marquand Books and D.A.P./Distributed Art Publishers have adroitly produced and distributed this book.

I am deeply grateful for the supporters of the exhibition and catalog: The Andy Warhol Foundation for the Visual Arts, the Conseil des arts et des lettres du Québec, the National Endowment for the Arts, and the Whitaker Foundation. *Hum* was made possible with the generous support of the Lahore Biennale Foundation and Portikus, Frankfurt.

It was a great pleasure to work with the deeply thoughtful and accomplished Hajra Waheed to bring this project to fruition. We are grateful to be able to share her significant, remarkable, and most relevant vision through the exhibition and publication.

The Spiral

HAJRA WAHEED

The spiral
is much more than just a form.

Its motion can be centrifugal and centripetal
it can denote both growth and decay
ascent and descent
evolution and involution
accumulation and dissolution.
It expands and contracts,
increases and decreases
reveals even as it hides
all the while offering back anew whatever it receives.

It is not amnesia nor the status quo.
It is not sapless nor atrophied.
It does not settle nor occupy.
It does not want you to believe it is immutable, inevitable,
invulnerable, unchangeable.
It is not naïvely cynical where perfection is a measure by which
all else falls short.
It is a study and not an art. Indeed it is not perfect.
It is a dance—of moving closer to the beloved
the possibility of approaching the essence
a way to understand and process time and space.

A rooted blade of grass circling around itself
it is the form of smoke entering the air
the reverberations of a drop of rain on another body of water.
The form of embryos and the cylindrical helices of our umbilical
cords that tether mother to child
of blooming date palms and the curvature of seashells.
It's the wave forms found in heart cells
rhythmically contracting to produce each beat
and the shape that nerve cells take before firing into the brain
at the slightest onset of fear.
The form DNA strands resume
that whirlpools inhabit
that fingerprints fortify.
The elliptical discs of spiral galaxies
the approach of a hawk to its prey
the approach of an insect to a source of light.
By maintaining the same shape through each successive turn
the least amount of energy is used.

It reverberates ad infinitum.

Informs our perspectives and grants us insight into what is
visible and invisible.
It is the practice of return.
It is never redundant.
It is the act of remembering,
the act of making oneself whole again.
At its eye, it is a compass that allows us to stand center in the
middle of a storm.
It reminds us that just as everything comes together
everything falls apart again.

It is standing in full knowledge of this and remaining
undefeated against despair.

It is a way of seeing.
The gift of wild possibilities and untold stories.
It is the belief that what we do matters.

It is made from the power and will of individuals and unarmed
people,
From the extraordinary achievement of ordinary people and
ordinary daily actions
of tending to, listening to, watching over and protecting.
It is survival as revival,
resistance as reclamation,
resilience as transformation.

It represents the awareness of the self
and the expansion of this awareness outwards.
It is about community
collaboration
attaching and being attached
about keeping an open heart
in the face of a broken one.

Change,
is rarely a straightforward line.

A Conversation between Hajra Waheed and Wassan Al-Khudhairi

WASSAN AL-KHUDHAIRI We are living in a time of crisis. There is a heightened sense of division around issues of ethnicity, religion, language, and nationalism, as well as the ongoing struggles of Indigenous people around the globe. Your work puts much of this into focus and invites viewers to engage, learn, and expand their connections to these conflicts and how they are lived. *A Solo Exhibition* positions *Hum* (2020) as the focal point of the exhibition. What prompted you to make this work?

HAJRA WAHEED What lives at the heart of this work—and what instigated both volumes of *Hum*—was a deep desire to be able to have people connect to and learn from, in a considered way, some really important social movements. There is a great deal of frustration with official politics and mainstream media given their inability to deal with the pressing problems of the world, and the lack of potential they have for challenging power in general. Social movements and community organizing have the capacity to take on power directly, and sound and song often play critical roles in this because of their ability to bring people together, to inspire and reinforce courage, especially at times when we're all feeling the full weight and scale of state violence and corporate power.

Hum was conceived in the wake of nationwide student solidarity marches in Pakistan against a major cut to the education budget and persistent violence against women on campuses. These erupted around the time of my site visit to Lahore in late November 2019 and coincided with a massive mobilization against the Citizenship (Amendment) Act across the border in India, which instituted discrimination against Muslims and other minorities. Both movements were nonviolent, but the government crackdowns were nevertheless brutal. The movements weren't in direct communication, and yet students took to the streets across both sides of the border in India and Pakistan reciting the same poetry and songs from revolutionary poets and political prisoners [Habib Jalib and Faiz Ahmed Faiz] from a previous generation. These were songs of struggle against state oppression, the rise of authoritarianism, and the plight and hopes of working people, the marginalized, and the dispossessed. What was apparent to me in that moment was the power of sound to not only transcend these lines of control but also act as a vehicle to reimagine our struggles and our future as a collective and borderless space.

After returning home, I came across other freedom movements and the story of Kurdish singer-songwriter Nûdem Durak's imprisonment. She received a nineteen-year sentence in Turkey for singing in the Kurdish language. My attempts to directly connect with her were unsuccessful, but her brother notified me that she had been sent to solitary confinement for rallying fellow inmates through song—the very act she was jailed for. I was told that even in solitary confinement she continued to defiantly hum. Durak's story became the impetus that led me to choose the medium of humming, which I initially conceived as a tool for street actions when singing lyrics can get you arrested. To orient the musical arrangers on both volumes who had never worked with humming, I asked them to imagine a thousand people walking shoulder to shoulder down the street and consider what would be required for us to teach them how to hum a song, whether it was familiar or not, within a span of a couple of minutes.

WA *Hum* also includes hummed songs by Faiz Ahmed Faiz, Habib Jalib, Sheikh Imam, Mohammed Wardi, and Hamid Hussain—musicians and poets who devoted and risked their lives to speak to struggles against abuses by the state. How and why did you choose these songs, and why do you think they continue to resonate in resistance movements today, even though many were written and performed decades ago?

HW All of these poets and singers have experienced imprisonment, as well as self-exile, for speaking out, and their songs suppressed or banned at various moments over the last decades. They all wrote and sang in the colloquial language of their familiarity—Rohingya, Urdu, Arabic, and, in the case of Wardi, Nubian—purposefully adopting a very simple style to address people and their concerns, and reach as wide an audience as possible.

In the cases of Faiz and Jalib, both were members of Pakistan's Progressive Writers' Association and actively spoke out against military coups, repressive regimes, and the stranglehold of capitalism in the country. Within *Hum*, there are two melodies from Jalib's poem "Dastoor" (The Constitution) and "Mein

Ne Usse Yeh Kaha," which loosely translates to "This Is What I Said to Him." Also included is Faiz's poem "Hum Dekhenge," which became widely popularized and reached iconic status when it was performed in song in 1986 by Iqbal Bano for fifty thousand people at Lahore Stadium in Pakistan. Gatherings of this sort were strictly forbidden under General Muhammad Zia-ul-Haq's dictatorship, but Bano's performance was nevertheless met with immense crowd support. She sang it a second time, but this time it was recorded, smuggled out, and distributed on bootleg cassette tapes across the country. The song has since become an unofficial anthem across both India and Pakistan for its ability to rally the masses towards struggles against state oppression.

Both Egyptian composer and singer Sheikh Imam and his longtime collaborator Ahmed Fouad Negm also sang in favor of the working classes, for social justice, and against exploitation, corruption, and dictatorship. Though their songs were banned on Egyptian radio and television stations, they gained immense popularity in the 1960s and 1970s. Revolutionary songs such as "Shayed Koussourak" (Erect Your Palaces) [featured in *Hum*] continue to live on in Egypt's occupied squares and embody the needs and vitality of people's movements across the Arab world and beyond. Much of this was due to the long-term and long-reach justice work by both throughout their lives, with Negm, for example, actively working at the Afro-Asian People's Solidarity Organization, a mass solidarity movement of the peoples of Africa and Asia united in a common struggle for the elimination of injustices and in defense against colonialism and racist policies.

Meanwhile, Wardi's career spanned over three hundred songs, with his first musical success achieved with a single deploring CIA complicity in the assassination of Congolese politician Patrice Lumumba in 1961. While his songs addressed Nubian folklore, revolution, and patriotism, politically he fought for social justice, decolonization, the redistribution of wealth, and Pan-Africanism. Wardi first performed "Hand Over the Keys to the Country" (penned by Sudanese poet Muhammad El-Makki Ibraheem) in 1997 during his exile following a military coup that placed the National Islamic Front in control of Sudan, making Colonel Omar al-Bashir president for over thirty years. The song has been revived many times over the years, most recently on the streets during Sudan's Revolution between 2017 and 2019 when al-Bashir was finally ousted.

Hamid Hussain is a Rohingya singer and songwriter who continues to live with his wife and son in a refugee camp in Buthidaung, Rakhine, one of the poorest states in Myanmar [Burma]. Since the government launched its genocide or so-called clearance operations in Rakhine State, populations continue to remain at grave risk of mass atrocities perpetrated by security forces and as a result of discriminatory laws and policies. Since August 2017, well over a million Rohingya have become refugees after fleeing brutal military crackdowns and being denied citizenship, all while facing multiple human rights abuses. Thousands have been left at sea after being turned away from Bangladesh and elsewhere. Bashir Ahmed was a Bangladeshi playback singer who started his career in the Pakistani film industry. His song "Thanda Thanda Bauiyaar" is cherished amongst the Rohingya community. Hussain (whose rendition of Ahmed's song was used as a reference in *Hum*'s composition) continues to defiantly sing and record in camp.

What's important to note here is that although all of these songs might arise out of specific historical circumstances, what prevents sounds like these from being purely of their time is that they resonate just as much with political struggles today as they did in the time when they were first written. In other words, they continue, in very real terms, to live through history and into the present because the struggles themselves are felt in mass by us all. This "We" in *Hum* is not anecdotal, it's the very thread that tethers us towards the kinds of mass mobilizations we require today, and which will ultimately continue to create far greater impact and more powerful change.

WA It makes sense that you chose the title *Hum*, but there's another layer to this—the word *hum* means "we" in Urdu. You originally made this work for a Lahore audience, so it's natural you would use your mother tongue and the most commonly spoken language in Pakistan. Urdu has a long and complex sociopolitical history in India and the subcontinent. Can you talk about its significance in the title for this work?

HW My sisters and I grew up with my father reciting Urdu *shayri* (poetry) to us at a very young age, and if we were lucky, he would recite his own prose when he felt compelled. It's common for my family (who is from Hyderabad, India) to sing and share Urdu poetry while together; it's how we gather and playfully exchange every day, whether at the dinner table or between chores or while exchanging stories late at night. When Hyderabad was annexed by the Indian military in 1948, upwards of forty thousand Muslims were killed in massacres, while countless others were displaced: this is a hidden history of Partition that hardly anyone discusses let alone knows about. At the same time, Hyderabad has had a long and rich global history connected to not only other places in India but also across the wider Indian Ocean world. However, since the definition of what it means to be Indian has also narrowed increasingly in recent years, Muslims in India, as well as the diaspora, are often interpreted as not belonging to India—a phenomenon that we see today taking very violent turns, with language, including Urdu, also being actively targeted and erased.

WA I find it compelling that you chose to have these songs hummed rather than sung. I know you're interested in exploring the idea of sonic agency—freedom of speech and our right to silence. As a sound we can make even when our mouths are closed, or for people under threat whose mouths have been forced shut, humming is a powerful tool. Can you talk more about humming and how you made the decision to use it as a tool for *Hum* and again in the more recent volume *Hum II* (2023)?

HW Humming is a meditation, phenomenon, and language. It's an utterance we're all capable of making, even when our lips have been sealed shut, and it can heal us when we've lost our voices altogether. We do it when we want to first memorize a song; we do it when we want to later remember it. We do it both consciously and subconsciously. It's incredibly legible yet insidious; it's irrefutable and infectious. Whether or not our mothers actively hummed to us as children isn't important; the fact is that as a medium it's been passed down ancestrally to all of us—and this is where its inherent power lies. Reimagined in this form, a song of resistance has the capacity to hold emancipatory potential, reaching beyond borders to encourage collective action.

WA For Sharjah Biennial 15 (2023) you created *Hum II*, which centers the voices of women in resistance movements. How do you see the second volume expanding and building upon the first?

HW In a number of social movements I was following in 2019, I could see that women's participation was critical to shaping these movements; they were clearly the driving force behind them. While the first volume focused on international solidarity movements between the 1960s and 1980s during processes of decolonization in the Global South, it haunted me that I had not shed light then on something that had been so glaring so early on in my process. This is essentially how the second volume came to be. It was guided by a deep deficit in the acknowledgment of the role that women consistently play at every level of societal and political transformation.

Consisting entirely of voice, *Hum II* features seven songs that have been central to popular uprisings, mass social movements, and anti-colonial struggles across the Americas, Africa, and Asia where women have been at the forefront. Many of these songs and musical forms have been either suppressed or banned; all of them are sung widely today, preserved and passed down by women to a new generation of youth. The composition begins with a K-pop hit by girl group Girls' Generation used by protesting female students and that also became the unofficial anthem for South Korea's Candlelight Revolution. The rest of the composition consists of two *taraweed*, an encrypted style of Palestinian folk song dating back to Ottoman-era conscription and now sung in protests against Israeli occupation; "Baraye," a viral song and anthem for Iran's current revolution composed by Iranian singer Shervin Hajipour in September 2022 following the death of Mahsa Amini; "Un violador en tu camino" (A Rapist in Your Path), a street action by Chilean feminist art collective LASTESIS that has been performed by tens of thousands of women across the world; and a *katajjaq*, a musical form and oral tradition of throat singing. Finally, the composition ends with a lullaby—a Bhim *palana*, or Bhim's cradle song, anti-caste songs composed, sung, and passed down by Dalit women to their children. The lullabies are used to transmit and popularize teachings of Bhimrao Ramji Ambedkar, who was known for having led India's anti-caste movement from the 1920s to the 1950s.

WA I find it fascinating that the composition ends with a lullaby, that is, a lullaby can also be a form of sharing knowledge and a form of resistance. What were you trying to convey with its inclusion?

HW I wanted to stress the importance of the role and voice of the mother in the production and transference of knowledge as the first site of resistance and of hope. *Hum II*'s composition purposefully ends by centering mothers in the fight to end three thousand years of caste apartheid. Ambedkar, who was himself a Dalit (previously known as "untouchable"), sought to demolish the tyrannies of Hinduism's caste system so as to rebuild a new social order based on the equality of all. He believed that this annihilation of caste could only proceed through the emancipation of women, particularly Dalit women. Today, Dalit women musicians such as Sheetal Sathe are bravely revitalizing this tradition of Ambedkari *jalsas* and Bhim *palanas* to bolster the anti-caste movement and denounce the new manifestations of caste emanating from the country's neoliberal regime and rise of Hindutva fascism. Their songs and the struggle to annihilate caste remain as critical as ever. Dalit women continue to face widespread discrimination, rampant sexual violence, and a severe lack of access to justice, education, health care, and other services. But these are ongoing struggles faced by not just women but also the 260 million Dalits across South Asia and its diaspora, struggles that cannot be seen as isolated, but rather entirely interconnected to other liberation struggles by Palestinian, Black, Indigenous, Latinx, femme, and queer communities.

WA *Hum II* also includes Inuit throat singing. You worked closely with Beatrice Deer and Sylvia Cloutier (both from Nunavik, the Northern Territories of Quebec), who included a unique piece for the composition. Can you expand on your decision to include throat singing?

HW Inuit throat singing, or *katajjaq* in Inuktitut, is a guttural form of chanting or musical performance that uses rhythmic inhalations and exhalations of breathing and reverberating in the throat to produce multiple notes simultaneously. Unlike other traditions of overtone singing in the world, katajjaq is practiced and passed down between women who initially developed it as a way to entertain themselves and their children during long winter nights when men were away hunting. It is performed typically as a playful duet in which two women face each other and exchange sounds and knowledges of the natural world, with one leading and the other repeating until one of them is unable to maintain the rhythm, tempo, or breathing pattern. Katajjaq can also be performed in communal gatherings of more than two women, as well as used to tell stories and as lullabies to soothe babies tucked close enough into the hoods of parkas to feel the vibration of their mother's throat.

Katajjaq was almost entirely lost due to a sustained program of cultural genocide pursued by the Canadian government and Christian missionaries after their arrival to Arctic communities in the late nineteenth century. Indigenous women are killed at nearly seven times the rate of non-Indigenous women in Canada. Meanwhile, the rate of violence experienced by Inuit women is fourteen times the national average, higher than that experienced by any other group of women in the country. Since the mid-1980s, throat singing has seen a resurgence, with elders passing down the form to a younger generation of Inuit women and girls who have returned to this long oral tradition and are exploring new ways of its expression. For these women, katajjaq is not only a powerful musical form but an act of love, healing, resistance, and decolonization.

In my exchanges with Beatrice and Sylvia about the other contributions that would go into this work, they felt called to also include their voices in the Chilean chant "Un violador en tu camino" by laying the bed track for it—a drumbeat—that the rest of the hummers followed along to. They inherently knew the importance and role of their voices in connecting, for example, the history of missing and murdered Indigenous and Aboriginal women to the global struggle against patriarchy and state and police violence.

WA For Beatrice and Sylvia to find inspiration in Chile's 2019 anti-austerity movement, where women's voices played such a critical role worldwide, is a great example of how solidarity across movements brings a larger voice to the struggles of many. What is the significance of "Un violador en tu camino"? What's the story behind this chant?

HW It's a powerful protest chant and dance routine that is synchronized to the beat of a drum. Translated from Spanish as "A Rapist in Your Path/Is You," "Un violador en tu camino" ironically references an old slogan portraying the police as "the friend in your path," and the lyrics call out the state for facilitating and condoning the use of sexual and other violence against the protesters. It was first performed on November 20, 2019, by a group of women from the feminist art collective LASTESIS and staged as a street performance in Valparaíso, Chile, amid a brutal repression of anti-austerity protests that had been taking place for weeks across the country. The performance was staged five days later in Santiago during a gathering to mark the International Day for the Elimination of Violence Against Women. Videos of this performance went viral and women began staging performances in over four hundred locations in over fifty countries, encouraging them to adapt the performance to their own contexts. In Chile itself, "Un violador en tu camino" was performed in cities, towns, and neighborhoods across the country by women of all ages during the protests of 2019 and 2020. The performance helped to center the feminist movement within the protest and its popular assemblies, and within the subsequent process to rewrite the national constitution that the protests achieved. On March 8, 2020, International Women's Day, nearly two million women marched in Chilean cities as part of a two-day General Feminist Strike, with groups of women performing "Un violador en tu camino" throughout the country.

WA The impact of *Hum* is evident when experiencing the work in person. In both volumes, you've created spaces that are almost like sanctuaries, offering an almost transcendental experience. In St. Louis during opening weekend, we saw visitors sit, lay, or meditate in the space—eyes closed—and many left the space eager to track you down to share their experiences. It was clear to me that people were affected by the work at a cellular level. Some of them shared with you stories of loss, others of joy, but the common sentiment was that they felt a sense of belonging. Can you elaborate on the spaces you've created and what's important for you in terms of what you want viewers to experience?

HW I've always been interested in creating diverse, informal yet collective listening experiences, from live radio to sit-ins to built environments. It's important to me to create safe spaces where visitors can feel held. There are many rituals to the architecture of space that can disarm and reengage us, whether it is the simple action of entering barefoot or allowing people to sit or lie down as they so choose. We inhabit spaces in so many different ways, so regardless of the context in which these volumes are experienced, it remains central for me to offer viewers the freedom to come as they are and be as they wish. Both volumes have a compositional arc and encourage a listening journey that is meant to activate our nervous systems. And if we are to stay long enough, we are capable of moving towards a feeling of release and catharsis, and, finally, perhaps towards a feeling that indeed we are all far more deeply interconnected as a species and far more powerful united together rather than separately.

WA What's clear in both volumes is that sound and poetry play pivotal roles in social movements, despite where they are happening in the world. It's a commonality across movements and cultures. The context for presenting *Hum* in St. Louis includes the city's history of resistance, including protest movements dating back to the 1800s and up to the ongoing Black Lives Matter movement, specifically in the wake of the police killing of Michael Brown. What are your reflections on siting *Hum* in St. Louis, which feels like a powerful act, against that historical backdrop?

HW I was deeply moved by the responses of the St. Louis community back in 2014, which in many ways became the steadfast beating heart of the Black Lives Matter front lines at an incredibly pivotal moment when global mobilization was taking root. The afternoon of Friday, June 5, 2020, also comes back to mind. I was in my studio in Montreal where just days before the streets below were flooded for the first time in months, as thousands of us marched against anti-Black police violence. I, like millions of people around the globe, had been consumed and inspired for ten days by national and international protests that erupted over the public lynching of another Black man—George Floyd—in the United States by police.

That afternoon, a public Zoom panel *Race at Boiling Point: The Fire This Time* organized by the University of California, Irvine gathered some of the most important thinkers and longtime organizers from the context of the United States—Angela Davis, Herman Gray, Gaye Theresa Johnson, Robin D. G. Kelley, and Josh Kun—to engage issues that had been further complicated and exposed by Covid-19 and global lockdown, issues such as the role of intersectional and international struggles at this time, the increased militarization of police and borders, racial capitalism, the feminist dimension of new social justice movements, and the power of the arts as a rallying force for imagining and sustaining solidarities. There have been many of these conversations since, but at that particular moment this one felt especially historic.

So many profound comments and insights were made that afternoon, but a couple that come to mind include Davis poignantly speaking to the importance of music, specifically the large role that Black music has played in conveying stories of Black resistance around the globe and how this has generated strong international solidarity for Black struggles in the United States. She went on to emphasize how critical such international solidarity remains to movements and this reconfirmed something I had been thinking about for years: the power, potential, and agency that can be found while sharing stories of resistance through music and sound across time and space.

Freedom struggles have to be broad, and reach across and challenge borders. We can't think of Black emancipation or women's liberation, for that matter, as being outside of or separate to larger struggles of oppression, just as we cannot truly be successful if our struggles can't be imagined as global. I do believe in the notion of building on the edge of each other's battles while simultaneously remaining conscious of the impacts of past and present experiences of inequality, trauma, and oppression, and a diversity of perspectives. It's not surprising that so many people in St. Louis have reached out to tell me how connected they finally feel, how not alone they are. Song and sound in these contexts have, time and time again, continued to generate not only a profound sense of felt meaning but also a declaration of shared visions, shared responsibilities, and shared futures.

WA Poetry is a form you continually engage with throughout your practice, and we see it appear in the exhibition with the work *We Need a Whole Lot of Trees* (2021). In contrast to the immersive, full-body experience of *Hum*, this work brings our attention to the crucial role of the natural world as the source of our existence—but in a much quieter, slower way. You created the work in collaboration with Taimoor Shahid, a multilingual poet, writer, scholar, translator, and your brother-in-law, and it presents your drawings and painted works alongside his poetry and inscriptions he translated from Urdu. What was this collaboration like? And what do you hope people take away from this work?

HW Collaborating with Taimoor is akin to the way two people find themselves talking for hours while walking through a forest. Conversations meander and our exchanges are easy, simple yet profound, playful, willing, and therefore always fruitful. Taimoor's poem "We Need a Whole Lot of Trees" (Humein Bahut Saare Darakht Chahiye) comes from a long tradition of protest poetry in South Asia, a form that continues to play a powerful role in social movements—and interestingly enough, something my sister Sarah, a historian of South Asia (and who also happens to be Taimoor's partner), wrote extensively about in her recent book, *Hidden Histories of Pakistan: Censorship, Literature, and Secular Nationalism in Late Colonial India* (2022), which examines the role left-leaning Muslim progressive writers like Habib Jalib and Faiz Ahmed Faiz played in freedom struggles against immense political suppression.

We Need a Whole Lot of Trees is a call to action and, like much of the work in the exhibition, a call that speaks to struggles that we are all collectively facing at planetary scales. While it continues to receive little attention from wealthy countries in the Global North, South Asia experiences some of the planet's worst climate catastrophes. Just last year, over a third of the entire country of Pakistan was under water.

This summer, India experienced soaring temperatures and catastrophic floods. Considered one of the world's most populous and poorest subregions, countries across South Asia are susceptible to gross food insecurity, displacement, and disease, not to mention the complete annihilation of their natural resources, water, lands, air, and forests. Here, climate change has induced the world's worst floods, droughts, and soaring temperatures over the last two years alone, creating irreversible consequences for the livelihoods and lives of millions upon millions of people. Last year's floods in Pakistan alone were so devastating that they affected over thirty-three million people. A report by ActionAid in 2020 estimates that the region, which has little to no infrastructures of support available, could see up to sixty-three million people forcibly migrating from the region by 2050 as a result of rising sea levels, cyclonic activity, and temperature changes.

In this context, *We Need a Whole Lot of Trees* reminds us not only of our sense of shared humanity but also of our many fundamental rights, including our rights to breathe and live in harmony with one another and all other living beings. After all, human existence today depends wholly on this very coexistence.

WA Your practice holds space for a multiplicity of media, each of which are interdependent on one another. Drawing and painting seem to form a foundational core for your practice. Your mother was a painter, you trained in painting and drawing, and you maintain a daily drawing practice. Can you expand on your painting practice? I'm interested in how your abstract paintings are a way for you to explore the mechanics of how we see.

HW If I were to imagine my multidisciplinary practice as a body, drawing would be my spine—a through line that tethers my practice—and painting would be my heart. It's fair to say that I've had a lifelong relationship to both. My mother was an abstract painter who stopped when I was born. She nor I ever thought in our wildest dreams that this would eventually become my life path. Both of us fought it. I wish she had never stopped. I'm sure it would have done her so much good. It's a way to process, a place to find stillness, and I think in many ways today I am grateful I also have this place I can go to do just that.

When we empty ourselves, we realize things about ourselves we previously may not have known. Abstract painting has a way of doing this, and every time I find myself compelled to approach it again, I am admittedly equal parts terrified and in awe. Although I studied in the advanced painting department at the School of the Art Institute of Chicago (SAIC) while receiving my BFA, it took me twelve years before I returned to it. It took me that long to kill whatever institutionalization of it that had disrupted my relationship to it. I always said to myself that if I ever were to return, I would start by painting the sea. That became *Our Naufrage 1–10* (2014). Since then, I've slowly been making my way back to it, painting in whatever style that comes out of me in the moment, from the magic realism of *Avow 1–38* (2017) to more recent abstract painted works like *Apparitions 1–18* (2021) and *Sound Studies* (2023).

WA While *Sound Studies 1–6* (2023), *Sound Studies 1–9* (2023), and *Studies for a Sound Chamber 1–9* (2023) are drawings and painted works on paper, they so clearly evoke sound. There's a sense of movement and action in their lines, and the titles suggest spaces where sound might echo or reverberate. *Flight in Form* (2019), a series of delicate white porcelain sculptures, seems to represent sound through visual form, and like the drawings they seem to provoke a sense of quiet movement. Why are you interested in creating forms to represent sound, something that seems so inherently intangible? Are these works an attempt at visualizing sound?

HW It sometimes takes me up to a year before I can begin talking about anything new I've made. I guess the best way I can answer this is, by approach, they were a series of meditations, meditations on sound. As a word, *sound* has many connotations for me; it's profoundly personal yet surprisingly social in that it has the ability to bring both the human and nonhuman together in communal and reciprocal entanglements. It has the ability to convey alternate realities and worlds, and it can do this in deeply sensorial and visual ways. We don't find ourselves closing our eyes and listening intently without reason. When we close one sensorial pathway, another opens. Sound doesn't have to be an aural experience. It becomes a portal calling visualization into focus and has the capacity to transport us, propelling us back in time or projecting us forward into futures that have yet to be realized. But to answer your question—yes, in brief, these works are an attempt at visualizing sound. Whether its final form is a line drawing or a fragile line of porcelain or multiple lines of speakers falling from the ceiling, I am quite certain that in some way or another, I am drawing sound in space.

All of these works were approached as exercises. In the case of each of the works in *Sound Studies 1–9*, for example, I hummed to myself while moving a full pen of ink on each page until the ink ran out.

WA In these works, it seems like you are asking the viewer to slow down, look closely, and listen carefully. Slowing down is the opposite message from what we typically receive in a world where everything moves so quickly and there's competition for our attention. Instead, your work seems to ask for patience from the viewer. That sort of demand for careful attention also occurs with *The Spiral* (2019), an immersive installation that bookends the exhibition. The spiral form is universal. It's a shape informed by nature and referred to in many cultures around the world as a representation of continuity. To experience this work, viewers enter a dark room where the film is projected and they become slightly disoriented. We're guided by your voice as you recite a poem about the form of a spiral. It took you two years to write this poem. Can you talk about how the words came to be? What is your relationship with the spiral form?

HW *The Spiral* was born out of a defining US election year in 2016 and the birth of my son, both of which brought with them a new set of existential questions. Spirals can be found in history, across space and throughout time, embedded deep into Indigenous knowledge the world over, in religious symbols and spiritual traditions, in art and literature, in folklore and mythology, science, mathematics, and nature. The spiral is all around us, existing within the fabric of our very DNA. A simple line that grows continuously toward or away from its own center. This line, this thread, this form—the spiral—manages to remain a metaphor, an archetypal symbol for cycles of life and death, and with that, growth and transformation.

US Election Day in 2016 had a particular resonance, as it happened to be the day my son was to be born. I was nine months pregnant and as fully prepared as I thought I could be—psychically, physically, emotionally. But then the results were announced. Trump had indeed won. I remember the day after very clearly, and the grief that people carried with them, even in Canada. Everyone I knew either called in sick or took a half day. I paced back and forth in the house for much of the day. I remember it was uncomfortable to sit, and I hoped that the gravitational pull of my pacing would work its magic and get my son positioned and moving into the world. In the days that followed, I soon realized this was only wishful thinking.

The news had profound implications, and as much as I tried to keep them at bay, this knowledge seeped into me at every level. A paralysis set in that even my new mother's instincts couldn't push away. Meanwhile, calls started pouring in. One by one, friends, many of them longtime community organizers, started arriving at our place, making their way around our kitchen table while we poured rounds of tea. They needed a long view and looked to my partner at the time to share his understanding of and relationship to social movements and the potential they have for radical change.

Ultimately, all of us grappled with trying to find a sense of hope in an avalanche of darkness that seemed to have descended that day. The kind of hope that Rebecca Solnit says is not a belief that everything was, is, or will be fine, but rather hope as an embrace for uncertainty, for the unknown and the unknowable, hope amidst the less visible long-term organizing and groundwork that often lays the foundation for change, hope that is "about broad perspectives with specific possibilities, ones that invite or demand that we act."

If there was anything that was clear in that moment, it was my desperate need, regardless of what was to come, to sift through and be able to find these openings. I needed it in order to birth my child and every day thereafter. I needed it for my practice, for our survival, for this crucial time on our planet. This meditation on this form became that search and marked the beginning of a journey of uncertainty *with hope*. Aside from the community of elders I've come to know over the years, for which I remain indebted to their wisdoms, I also remain indebted to those forms found in our natural world, including the spiral, that remind us every day of the manifold ways we can imagine and reimagine ourselves in relation to change and transformation, even as we continue to grapple with our histories and heal from them so that it may lead to some kind of justice work.

WA You pursued an MA and a PhD in education. Do you think that training set the foundation for your interest in making work that is rooted in a deep desire to help people connect and learn about social movements?

HW I've been making art for over twenty years out of school, but to be honest, it took me over a decade before I was willing to call myself an artist. Before that, I would only introduce myself as an educator, and if nudged in the moment by friends who knew me well, I would reluctantly divulge that I also happened to paint. While I was obtaining a BFA at SAIC, I began working across the south and west sides of the city as an arts facilitator in a program for adults living with autism and Down syndrome that was started by a couple of friends. Those first two and a half years opened up a world to me, and I spent many years after building curriculums and teaching, eventually full-time throughout my MA and after pursuing a PhD in international and comparative education. (A PhD that, admittedly, I quit rather than completed after four years of going into debt while studying, from the inside, the impacts of neoliberal policies and practices on higher education.)

Many of my teaching interests had always centered around alternative, popular, and informal education movements. So I quickly fell into the work of Paulo Freire, a Brazilian philosopher, activist, and educator who worked closely with workers and peasant groups in Brazil and Chile. After being forced to flee Brazil following a military coup, he wrote *Pedagogy of the Oppressed* while in exile in Chile in the late 1960s. It's a revolutionary reformulation of the very idea and purpose of schooling, a seminal text and path forward that centered education as a source for critical consciousness and liberation rather than oppression. It's a powerful work that centers humanization and liberation as a collective effort, a book that has been banned at various moments over the last half century, including in apartheid South Africa, parts of Latin America, and even in the state of Arizona in 2012 by right-wing policymakers who considered it to "promote the overthrow of the US government." I became very interested and involved in Freire's work and worlds and was later co-supervised by one of his longtime collaborators and comrades, Donaldo Macedo, a linguist, educator, and Freire's translator of his many texts, including *Pedagogy of the Oppressed*. I'm quite certain that my continued interest in social movements and the justice work that can be had through the medium of education has been deeply inspired by so many humans I've come across over the years and had the honor to work with. I'm also quite certain that all of my work, both inside the classroom but mostly outside it, whether in my practice or in life in general, has been informed in some way by these ways of worldmaking.

As an artist and educator, I really believe in the role that the arts can play in creating, encouraging, and sustaining *affective* experiences—social movements cannot sustain themselves without this, without continually nurturing ways to keep people emotionally connected and invested in larger struggles. The arts have the capacity for establishing new terms and creating new lexicons that might be useful to continuing to mobilize for and build social movements, and I suppose this is something that continues to remain a deep interest and exploration of mine.

WA How has your life experience informed your views on the current climate of the world? What are your hopes for the future?

HW I come from generations of ancestors who moved between and across borders, made and left homes behind for the prospects of work and the possibilities of a new life, sacrificed or followed love, and brought with them new folds of family. I approach my work by tracing these lines back, and these stories have become inflection points that inform and guide my own experiences and positionalities of being a person from the global majority with complex ties and relationships to North America, the Middle East, and South Asia—having been born of Muslim Indian immigrant parents.

Most of us come from deeply complex histories and ties. We were born from those who pushed against systems of injustice or moved alongside them. We were born from those who shied away from, or resisted and spoke out against, the abuses they suffered and/or were liberated from. The artists I have been so fortunate to come to know deeply have come to their practices with both the melancholy of these ancestral knowledges and the deep desire to carry forth a spirit of resilience, to challenge themselves in spite of it all, while spending their lives doing the less visible long-term justice work that I spoke of earlier. Our work is to make right what we can, fight for one another, and feed hope—for ourselves, for each other, for the children.

ہمیں بہت سارے درخت چاہئیں

ہمیں بہت سارے درخت چاہئیں

جیسے ہارسنگھار کا درخت

جس سے ہم اپنے عزیزوں کے مقبرے آباد کر سکیں

کہ صبح کو انکی قبروں پر

بہت سے پھول اکھٹے ہو جائیں

ہمیں بہت سارے درخت چاہئیں

جیسے جامن کا درخت

جسکی مظبوط لکڑی سے

ہم وہ کشتیاں بنا سکیں

جن پہ ہمیں سمندر میں جھونک دیا جائے گا

ہمیں بہت سارے درخت چاہئیں

جیسے پالاش کا درخت

جسکی پتیوں سے ہم تشتریاں بنائیں

تا کہ ہوٹلوں میں ٹوٹنے والی قیمتی پلیٹوں پر

بیروں کو نوکریاں نا کھونی پڑیں

We Need A Whole Lot of Trees

TAIMOOR SHAHID

ہمیں بہت سارے درخت چاہئیں

جیسے بیل کا درخت

جسے شنکر نے لکشمی کی

بجھائی ہوئی کومل آنکھ سے پیدا کیا

ہمیں اس بیل کا پھل چاہیے

جس سے

ہمیں بہت سارے درخت چاہئیں

جیسے اشوک کا درخت

جسکے پھول کو محبت کے دیوتا کام دیو نے

پانچ تیروں میں شامل کیا تھا

ہمیں اشوک کے پھول چاہئیں

ہمیں بہت سارے درخت چاہئیں

جیسے نیم کا درخت

جسکے نیچے بیٹھ کر

ہم کچھ دیر آرام کر سکیں

ہمیں بہت سارے درخت چاہئیں

جیسے کدالی کا درخت

جس کے لمبے پتوں سے

ہم اپنی عریانی ڈھانک سکیں

ہمیں بہت سارے درخت چاہئیں

جیسے بیری کا درخت

جسکی لکڑی سے

ہم درانتی بنا سکیں

جو انقلاب کے جھنڈے سے

گر چکی ہے

ہمیں بہت سارے درخت چاہئیں

جیسے برگد کا درخت

جسکی کومل پتیوں سے

ہم اپنے کوڑھ کا علاج کر سکیں

We Need A Whole Lot of Trees

translated from Urdu by
TAIMOOR SHAHID

We need a whole lot of trees
like the tree of Night Jasmine
with which we line
the tombs of our friends
so that each morning
their graves are covered
in fragrant flowers

We need a whole lot of trees
like the tree of mangrove
with whose good timber
we build the boats
in which we'll be thrust
into open seas

We need a whole lot of trees
like the flame-of-the-forest
with whose wide leaves
we fashion plates
so that waiters in fancy hotels
don't lose jobs
over broken china

We need a whole lot of trees
like the herbaceous banana
with whose long leaves
we cover our nakedness

We need a whole lot of trees
like the tree of jujube
from whose hard timber
we carve the sickle
that has long fallen
from the flag of revolution

We need a whole lot of trees
like the tree of banyan
with whose tender leaves
we treat our leprosy

We need a whole lot of trees
like the tree of golden apple
which Shankar created
from Lakshmi's blinded eye
we need the fruit of the golden apple
with which we anoint the wounds
of those afflicted by snake bites

We need a whole lot of trees
like the tree of sorrow-less Ashok
whose flower the God of Love Kamdev
included in his five arrows of desire
we need Ashok's flower

We need a whole lot of trees
like the tree of Neem
under whose soothing shade
we sit and rest awhile

The Song of Songs
On Hajra Waheed's *Hum*

Music can be the ultimate circumvention.
Even if it's forbidden, it finds a way.[1]

— MICHAEL RAKOWITZ

RAYYA BADRAN

I first listened to *Hum* (2020) in late 2020 on Radio al Hara during *Listening with Reem Shadid*, a show hosted by Palestinian curator and writer Reem Shadid. The online radio station, which was created by five friends (Elias and Yousef Anastas, Yazan Khalili, Saeed Abu-Jaber, and Mothanna Hussein) and started broadcasting in Bethlehem, Ramallah, and Amman, quickly joined a growing roster of stations broadcasting from different cities across the Mediterranean and West Asia. Grappling with the isolation wrought by the pandemic, Radio al Hara's listening audience grew, allowing us to experience singular moments of collective listening during a period of confinement and solitude. A new topography of radio in the region was drawn through which one could imagine its future potentialities in an increasingly fractured area. These recent communal experiments with radio not only summoned us to listen, alone and together, but also harnessed a sense of transnational collectivity through the ever-expanding medium of sound. In its three years of existence, Radio al Hara has regularly become a site of sonic and musical protests through which musicians and artists across continents expressed solidarity against forms of injustice and oppression.

These new informal and communal stations are significant insofar as they embody a sort of renaissance for the medium itself but also in furthering listening practices for audiences who don't find themselves in the outmoded state or private FM and AM radio systems. The audience, in fact, has become the producer, the programmer, the DJ, and the show host; in short, the maker of these stations. There is an invaluable cultural and political potential for us to preserve and move forward with in the future, especially when we consider the history of radio in many parts of the Global South, which was introduced by colonial powers. The music, conversations, political speeches, and sounds coming out of living rooms in Beirut, Tunis, Bethlehem, and other cities have helped cement new solidarities and foster artistic collaborations, creating more expansive and critical spaces for collective listening.

First exhibited at the Lahore Biennale 02 in 2020, *Hum* is a sixteen-channel musical composition and installation that weaves together hummed renditions of songs written and sung by imprisoned or exiled writers, poets, musicians, and political activists from South, Central, and West Asia, and East and North Africa. While my experience of *Hum* was ex situ and in stereo, it was one of the most arresting moments I have had with a work of art in a long time. I tuned in to listen to *Hum* from my home in Beirut and was overcome by the emotive force of the composition and an acute awareness of the presence of others listening in. I would even argue that while Waheed conceived the installation as a piece in which light and physical space play a crucial role in our experience of it—what the artist calls "architecture of ritual"—the communal space of radio, broadcasting via Bethlehem made the experience of listening more potent and moving.[2] Prior to this broadcast, Waheed played excerpts of the piece in other audio interviews, but it was on Radio al Hara that *Hum* played in its entirety before a radio audience. The digital realm replaced the large audience halls of Lahore Fort's Diwan-i-Aam, where it was first shown; both venues were conceived as open spaces through which individuals could transcend physical and political borders at critical junctures of history. Waheed's commitment to carving a space for what she calls "abolitionist modes of listening" was fulfilled during this broadcast. The artist pointed out the similarity between this mode of listening and the gesture of taking one's shoes off before entering a space: "a ubiquitous yet profound gesture that tends to shape the ways we enter a space, how we might listen in a space that is not our own, how we might understand, commune, or participate."[3] There was a reversal of participation at play during *Hum*'s radio broadcast. The piece played back in a space that had become our own, a space that summoned us to listen collectively. Radio al Hara was a new radiophonic terrain untethered from wave frequencies, a new shared space made by and for people long deprived of mobility, communion, and freedom. The composition —a composite of silenced voices—instilled a sense of communality and attention rarely felt in the drawn-out aftermath of successive revolutionary defeats.

Against forgetfulness

According to literary scholar Steven Connor, "the hum, like the whisper . . . seems expressive, but impersonal. Humming is a background rather than foreground phenomenon. We hum distractedly and as accompaniment rather than with full and conscious intent, humming typically being something we do when pleasurably absorbed in something else."[4] Looking into the diverse functions and meanings of humming sounds made by humans, insects, and machines, Connor evokes how psychoanalysts have interpreted the ways humans use humming "as a filler for songs the words of which are not known" and that are suppressed or avoided as a result of unsettled emotions.[5] Wanting to go beyond the psychoanalytic explanation, the author concludes:

> *the hum might be better regarded as the articulation of nasality that otherwise lies hidden beneath and within all articulation, as its binding and enlivening principle. The hum is the melodic inner lining of all speech, a song that never quite bursts into song, nor even fully differentiates individual melodies (which all sound much of a muchness when they are hummed), but is rather the song of songs, the average and the aggregation of all the tunes that lie latent within the voice.*[6]

The last sentence seems to encapsulate the political and aesthetic project underlying Waheed's *Hum* series because it also challenges the indistinctness with which Connor characterizes the hum. In Waheed's body of work, humming resists forgetfulness; it is an act that guarantees that songs of past struggles will remain in the airways of those who hum them, even after words are lost or fail the ones who speak them.

Helmed by Waheed and a team of audio, technical, and architectural engineers, and musical arrangers, these songs are written anew so that they may be recognizable to listeners without the help of musical accompaniment or voice, but they are also weaved together so seamlessly—a tapestry of sustained breathing—that their sequence seems to flow almost naturally. The affective, aesthetic, and political qualities are contained by the air that circulates in the bodies of the anonymous performers. In an interview with artist Reece Cox, Waheed posits a distinct and poetic approach to humming, one which assigns the bilabial sound to forms of radical resistance against the silencing of songs. Rather than being distraction or ambivalence, the hum is:

> *incredibly legible, yet insidious, it's irrefutable and infectious. We do it when we want to first memorize a song, we do it when we want to later remember it. We do it both consciously and subconsciously. It's an utterance that actively lives in the cracks and between spaces—and this is what I was most interested in, more importantly, where I wanted the work to live.*[7]

Hum does not merely reproduce popular revolutionary songs from distant pasts but considers who sings them today and where. Waheed's selected songs are a testament to the perennial relevance of past struggles and mass movements in the face of occupation but also military and state oppression. *Hum* begins and ends with songs once performed by Nûdem Durak, a Kurdish singer and teacher whose political songs landed her in prison. Waheed has said the piece "continues to act as a tribute to her continual resistance to being silenced."[8]

Hum II (2023) thus begins where its predecessor ended, with songs of resistance transmitted by women at the forefront of social and political struggles in places like South Korea, Palestine, Iran, and India across generations. While both compositions possess a solemn quality, *Hum II* feels more exuberant and celebratory at times, insisting that joy also underlines many women's movements as they continue to sing and transmit these songs through generations in distinct contexts and struggles. One stark difference in the performance of *Hum II* is the inclusion of other wordless vocalities; for example, Inuit throat singing or *katajjaq* from Nunavik, Quebec, a chant and performance sung by women that typically mimics the sounds of water, animals, and everyday noises, permeates the latter section of the piece. In both compositions, the labor of breathing is rendered audible, grounded in bodies that unite in both song and struggle for equality and freedom, for love and pleasure. Audible gasps for air, often bordering on whispers, can be heard.

Waheed's *Hum* series gives shape to a sonorous heritage excavated from the cavities of our own bodies. Both the practice of listening and the culture of song have long existed in the fractured geographies the artist invokes in the conversation of hums. By humming, one cannot silence that which cannot be spoken. It circumvents prisons, walls, physical and imagined borders, and languages; it draws new geographies entwined by the sustained breaths of people who may forget the words but never forget the people who have sung them.

NOTES

1. Michael Rakowitz, *I'm good at love, I'm good at hate, it's in between I freeze*, ed. Anthony Downey (London: Sternberg Press, 2019), 151.

2. Hajra Waheed and Reece Cox, "Hajra Waheed: Abolitionist Modes of Listening," *Contemporary Journal* 3 (December 21, 2020), https://thecontemporaryjournal.org/strands/sonic-continuum/info-unltd-special-hajra-waheed-on-hum-and-abolitionist-modes-of-listening.

3. Waheed and Cox, "Hajra Waheed: Abolitionist Modes of Listening."

4. Steven Connor, *Beyond Words: Sobs, Hums, Stutters and Other Vocalizations* (London: Reaktion Books, 2014), 92.

5. Connor, *Beyond Words*, 94.

6. Connor, *Beyond Words*, 94–95.

7. Waheed and Cox, "Hajra Waheed: Abolitionist Modes of Listening."

8. Waheed and Cox, "Hajra Waheed: Abolitionist Modes of Listening."

Apparitions of the Lost, and of the Found

H.G. MASTERS

[1]
The words.
The sun's energy, at 3.846×10^{26} watts per second.
A woman.
Farmers, and their land.
Sometime in the night.
*

[2]
Pigments, dispersed in water.
Many women.
Young men, taken from their homes in the middle of the night.
The original translation.
Imperceptibly over time.
*

[3]
Trees, and the flowers that they would have dropped.
A generation of young girls.
Direction.
Individuals' voices.
After the first ship arrived in the bay.
*

[4]
A sense of ourselves.
The hours of daylight.
Those who remain silent.
Countries.
When the first galaxies were born.
*

[5]
Distinct shapes.
The house you once slept in.
The last native speaker.
Breath.
In the silence before dawn.
*

[6]
A metal sphere, 1.5 meters in diameter.
Fishermen, with their nets.
Parcels of land.
The still surface of the water.
Before turning the page.
*

[7]
Ways of living.
Children, and their childhoods.
Those who must leave.
The faithful—and with them, their faith.
At the moment the sun set.
*

[8]
Men, walking through the desert at night, away from the city lights.
A single page.
Memories from before your birth.
Passages of return.
Amid a torrential rainstorm.
*

[9]
Boats full of people, with their children, in the sea.
Tiles from the wall.
The narrator.
How we used to speak.
While she was imprisoned.
*
[10]
A clear view of the stars.
A handwritten letter.
Free movement.
The borders of a painting.
When we began synchronizing time.
*
[11]
The forcefully relocated.
Millions of books.
Eyes.
Seasonal rains.
As they were beating them.
*
[12]
The community that used to live there.
Air that is clean.
Those who must remain.
The memory of how things were.
Ultimately.

Apparitions of the Found

[1]
The woman, decades later.

A concise phrase, in an elaborate description.

Your cousin, who left home months ago.

Countless shades of blue.

Under the cover of darkness.

*

[2]
Bodies, together.

A place to sleep while traveling over land.

The first person ever to sing.

The meaning you were looking for.

Once the regime fell.

*

[3]
A bus full of students.

Detainees attempting to escape.

The bottom of the sea.

The original author, centuries after they died.

Singing amid the surging crowd.

*

[4]
The [un]officially disappeared.

A color faded by the sun.

The specific coordinates.

Lights off in the distance.

As the image comes into focus.

*

[5]
A single movement of the arm.
A fresh-running stream.
The one who understands.
Stars ever farther back in time.
In the transition.
*

[6]
Brushstrokes, as the paint slowly dries.
The couple hiding under the bridge.
A view of the horizon.
The previous inhabitants.
As a mother puts her child to sleep.
*

[7]
The sensation that had eluded you.
Tantric painting, in Rajasthan.
Faded photographs of unknown people and places.
The few still living in the village.
When reaching out to one another.
*

[8]
The swelling of voices.
A satellite moving steadily across the sky.
Drifting in the open water.
New formations of the self.
Right where they should have been.
*

[9]

Long-forgotten melodies.

Ways of being together.

Partially redacted documents.

The feeling of embrace.

Before the start of the growing season.

*

[10]

Your descendants.

Particles in continuous motion.

Acts of recovery, and recovering.

Their own voices.

After the flood waters receded.

*

[11]

The last sliver of light.

Videos from the demonstration.

Resonances within and without.

A single sustained note.

Surrounded by friends and strangers.

*

[12]

The formless form.

Our unfolding futures.

The last warmth from the fire's embers.

A gradual stripping away.

At the moment of conception.

Biographies

HAJRA WAHEED's multidisciplinary practice ranges from painting and drawing to video, sound, sculpture, and installation. Amongst other issues, she explores the nexus between security, surveillance, and the covert networks of power that structure lives, while also addressing the traumas and alienation of displaced subjects affected by legacies of colonial and state violence. Characterized by a distinct visual language and unique poetic approach, her works often use the ordinary as a means to convey the profound, and landscape as a medium to transpose human struggle and a radical politics of resistance and resilience.

Her recent exhibitions worldwide include: Haus der Kulturen der Welt, Berlin (2023); Sharjah Biennial 15, Sharjah (2023); Contemporary Art Museum St. Louis, MO (2023); State of Concept Athens, Greece (2023); PHI Foundation for Contemporary Art, Montreal (2021); Portikus, Frankfurt (2020); Centre Pompidou, Paris (2020); Lahore Biennale 02, Pakistan (2020); British Museum, London (2019); The Power Plant Contemporary Art Gallery, Toronto (2019); 57th Venice Biennale, Venice (2017); 11th Gwangju Biennale, South Korea (2016); Baltic Centre for Contemporary Art, Gateshead, United Kingdom (2016); KW Institute for Contemporary Art, Berlin (2015); La Biennale de Montréal, Musée d'art contemporain de Montréal, Quebec (2014); Herbert F. Johnson Museum of Art, Ithaca, NY (2012); and Fundació Antoni Tàpies, Barcelona (2012).

She is a recipient of the Sharjah Biennial 15 Prize (2023), Hnatyshyn Foundation Award (2022), Victor Martyn Lynch-Staunton Award (2014) for outstanding achievement as a mid-career artist, and a finalist for the Sobey Art Award (2016). Waheed's works can be found in permanent collections, including the Museum of Modern Art, New York; British Museum, London; National Gallery of Canada, Ottawa; Centre Pompidou, Paris; Art Institute of Chicago, IL; Burger Collection, Zurich/Hong Kong; and Devi Art Foundation, New Delhi.

WASSAN AL-KHUDHAIRI is the former Ferring Foundation Chief Curator at the Contemporary Art Museum St. Louis, where she organized exhibitions and commissions with artists Gala Porras-Kim, Martine Gutierrez, Derek Fordjour, Stephanie Syjuco, Shara Hughes, Paul Mpagi Sepuya, Bethany Collins, Lawrence Abu Hamdan, Guan Xiao, and Hayv Kahraman, among others. She co-produced the podcast *Radio Resistance* to accompany the exhibition and publication *Stories of Resistance* (2021), a thematic group show with over twenty participating artists. Al-Khudhairi is currently curating the 2025 Hawai'i Triennial.

Al-Khudhairi was co-curator of the 6th Asian Art Biennial in Taiwan in 2017 and co–artistic director for the 9th Gwangju Biennale in South Korea in 2012. She served as the Hugh Kaul Curator of Modern and Contemporary Art at the Birmingham Museum of Art, where she organized the first large-scale exhibition of the museum's contemporary collection, *Third Space / shifting conversations about contemporary art* (2017). Serving as the founding director of Mathaf: Arab Museum of Modern Art in Qatar, Al-Khudhairi oversaw the opening of the museum in 2010, co-curated the exhibition *Sajjil: A Century of Modern Art* (2010), and curated *Cai Guo-Qiang: Saraab* (2011).

She holds a BA in art history from Georgia State University and an MA in Islamic art and architecture with distinction from the School of Oriental and African Studies in London. Al-Khudhairi is a graduate of the Getty Leadership Institute, the recipient of the 2021 VIA Curatorial Fellowship Grant, and a fellow in the 2021 Center for Curatorial Leadership program.

Based in Beirut, **RAYYA BADRAN** is a writer, editor, and translator whose practice centers on sound, music, and contemporary art. Her writings have been featured in various publications, such as *Bidoun*, *ArtReview*, *Art Papers*, *Norient*, *The Wire*, and more. She was guest editor of the Beirut Art Center's online publication *The Derivative* in 2020 and curator and editor of the *Norient City Sounds Online Special: Beirut* in 2022. She taught courses on contemporary art and sound studies in the Department of Fine Arts and Art History at the American University of Beirut from 2014 to 2021. She is co-curator of the second edition of the Listening Biennial in 2023.

H.G. MASTERS is a writer and deputy editor and deputy publisher at *ArtAsiaPacific* magazine in Hong Kong. He has been an editor at *ArtAsiaPacific* since 2007 in various roles, including editor of the annual *ArtAsiaPacific Almanac*, a survey of the year in art from across Asia. Masters is the co-editor of ArtAsiaPacific Foundation books, including curator and art historian David Elliott's collected writings on artists from Asia, *Art and Trousers: Tradition and Modernity in Contemporary Asian Art* (2021). He was the guest editor of *The Making of M+* (Thames & Hudson, 2021) in collaboration with designers Sulki and Min. Additionally, he has written catalog essays about artists including Pacita Abad, Ha Chong-Hyun, Haegue Yang, Shinro Ohtake, Hajra Waheed, Monir Shahroudy Farmanfarmaian, and Halil Altindere, among others. His essays and reviews have been published in magazines and journals in New York, London, Istanbul, and Beirut.

Exhibition Checklist

All works by Hajra Waheed, courtesy the artist

The Spiral, 2019
Video installation
7:10 minutes

Flight in Form, 2019
Porcelain
Dimensions variable

Hum, 2020
Multichannel sound installation with custom speakers
36:17 minutes

Hum: Studies for a Sound Chamber, 2020
Etching on paper
13 ½ × 10 ½ inches framed

Apparitions 1–18, 2021
Pigment in Gum Arabic binding on 100% cotton Arches watercolor paper
15 ½ × 12 inches framed, each of 10
15 ½ × 20 inches framed, each of 4

Studies for a Sound Chamber 1–9, 2023
Ink on paper
13 ½ × 10 ½ inches framed, each of 9

We Need a Whole Lot of Trees 1–10, 2023
Ink on paper, including a poem written and translated from Urdu by Taimoor Shahid
10 ½ × 13 ½ inches framed, each of 10

Sound Studies 1–6, 2023
Oil stick and acrylic on paper
17 ¾ × 18 inches framed, each of 6

Sound Studies 1–9, 2023
Oil stick and acrylic on paper
13 ½ × 10 ½ inches framed, each of 9

Untitled 1–2, 2023
Pigment in Gum Arabic binding on linen
24 × 32 inches framed, each of 2

Published on the occasion of the exhibition *Hajra Waheed: A Solo Exhibition*, at Contemporary Art Museum St. Louis, September 8, 2023–February 11, 2024, curated by Wassan Al-Khudhairi, former Ferring Foundation Chief Curator, with Misa Jeffereis, Associate Curator.

Major support for *Hajra Waheed: A Solo Exhibition* is provided by The Andy Warhol Foundation for the Visual Arts and the Conseil des arts et des lettres du Québec. This exhibition is generously supported in part by the National Endowment for the Arts and the Whitaker Foundation.

The Andy Warhol Foundation for the Visual Arts

NATIONAL ENDOWMENT for the ARTS
arts.gov

Hum was made possible with the generous support of the Lahore Biennale Foundation and Portikus, Frankfurt.

CONTEMPORARY ART MUSEUM ST. LOUIS
3750 Washington Boulevard
St. Louis, MO 63108
camstl.org

Produced by Marquand Books, Seattle
marquandbooks.com

Editor: Wassan Al-Khudhairi
Designer: Ryan Polich
Associate editor: Graham Eng-Wilmot
Typesetter: Maggie Lee
Proofreader: Carrie Wicks
Printer: die Keure, Belgium

All contributions © the authors
First Edition © 2024 Contemporary Art Museum St. Louis

All rights reserved. No part of this book may be reproduced or transmitted in any form or by any means, electronic or mechanical, including photocopy, recording, or any other information storage and retrieval system, or otherwise without written permission from the publishers.

ISBN: 978-0-9977364-4-1

Available through D.A.P./Distributed Art Publishers
75 Broad Street, Suite 630
New York, NY 10004
212.627.1999
artbook.com

Contemporary Art Museum St. Louis
Board of Directors

Officers
Jackie Yoon, Chair
Paul Cambridge, Vice Chair
Joe Herman, Treasurer
Terry Hoffmann, Secretary

Members
Bradley Bailey
David Bentzinger
Larnise Boain
Candice Carter-Oliver
Gail E. Childs
Sylvester Chisom
Jane Clark
Alexis Cossé
Preston Davis
JiaMin Dierberg
John Ferring
Shereen Fischer
Nancy Kranzberg
Hedwig Lee
Judith W. Levy
Emily Rauh Pulitzer
Jacob Reby
Julian Schuster
Rick Shang
Rex A. Sinquefield
Andrew Srenco
Michael Staenberg
Donald Suggs
Kate Warne
Pat Whitaker
Tracie Wolfmeyer

Emeritus
Susan Barrett
Barbara Z. Cook
Charles Cook
Terrance J. Good
Marylen L. Mann
Isabelle Montupet
Ann R. Ruwitch

CAM
Contemporary Art
Museum St. Louis